Emotional Intelligence

The Ultimate Guide for Cognitive Behavioral Therapy (CBT), How to Analyze People, Success at Work, Better Life & Relationships with Positive Psychology Mindset Coaching 2.0

Introduction

Congratulations on downloading *Emotional Intelligence 2.0: The Ultimate Mastery Guide for Cognitive Behavioral Therapy (CBT), Increasing Self Confidence, Discipline and EQ with Positive Psychology Mindset Coaching (Book series #2)* and thank you for doing so.

The following chapters will discuss the field of emotional intelligence, its history, and its importance in today's society. This book will also cover how emotional intelligence can be increased through self-confidence, discipline and mindset coaching. Within these pages you will find actionable techniques to increase your emotional intelligence and have the self-discipline to complete your projects and see your goals until the end.

There are plenty of books on this subject on the market, thanks again for choosing this one! Every effort was made to ensure it is full of as much useful information as possible, please enjoy!

Chapter 1: What is Emotional Intelligence?

Most people have never heard of emotional intelligence. And they definitely wouldn't know its importance in today's society. Emotional intelligence is so important that having it or a lack of having it affects every relationship in your life; personally and professionally. Emotional intelligence is your ability to recognize your emotions and the impact they have on others and being able to regulate those emotions in your daily relationships. Also emotional intelligence is the ability to read the emotions of the people around you, understand how these emotions affect them, empathize with the people around you and be able to handle relationships appropriately.

Five Components of Emotional Intelligence

Emotional intelligence has five different components as was identified by Goleman in 1995. His book *Emotional Intelligence* goes into great detail about these needed components. A weakness or lack of proficiency in either of these key areas will impact your relationships negatively. Let's take a closer look. The five components of emotional intelligence are:

- Self-awareness

- Self-regulation

- Motivation

- Empathy

- Social Skills

Self-awareness is the first and most important step in increasing your emotional intelligence. You cannot begin to establish and regulate relationships with others if you don't know yourself. When you become self-aware, you know how you feel, what has made you feel that way, and how your actions can affect the people around you in your personal life, as well as your professional life.

A person who is self-aware can also identify his strengths and weaknesses and know exactly how to use each to get the desired positive results needed to complete tasks successfully. His weaknesses don't scare him or cause him to shy away from others but he knows how to capitalize on his weakness and use his strengths to build solid relationships around him.

You might be asking, how a person can increase his self-awareness. One of the things that can improve your self-awareness skills is identifying your emotional triggers. Everyone has triggers. But sometimes it is hard to identify them because they are deeply imbedded into your psyche. If you know what triggers you, then you can re-route the negative energy when it takes place and alter the way you react to those triggers in a more positive way. Keeping a daily journal is another way to keep track of situations and circumstances that happen throughout your day. You can reflect on how these events made you feel, how you responded to them, what the results were, and how you can improve by reacting differently if similar situations should arise. Write all of these dynamics in your journal so that you can really analyze situations properly. There is nothing like a good visual to drive home the reality of a circumstance.

This leads us to the second most important step to increasing your emotional intelligence; self-regulation. It is not enough to be aware of your emotions. You must know how to regulate them. The way you respond to your triggers on a consistent basis determines the strength of your relationships. You must know how to respond to others whether it is in your personal life, the arena of academia, or in the workplace. There are a few practices that will assist you in increasing your self-regulation skills:

- Slow down, step back

- Remove yourself

- Consider the Consequences

Often when you are being triggered emotionally you react instantaneously and explosively. You may not always be fully aware that you are being triggered. So you have to learn to identify your triggers. You never want to react but rather you want to respond to the emotions in your life. In order for you to change this behavior, you have to fight the urge to react immediately. Although this immediate response is your need for instant gratification, it is almost always the incorrect response. In these cases you have to physically and mentally slow down and take a step back to observe the situation. Ask yourself why the emotion you are feeling is so strong? Why does this emotion produce this reaction and cause you to react without any caution.

If necessary completely detach or remove yourself from the situation physically or mentally. Give yourself time to identify what preferences aren't being met. What is it that you prefer to happen? For example, you want dishes cleaned and dinner ready when you come home from work. You walk in and these things are not done. This is your preference. But you also have to be flexible in life. You could exercise more patience and you can also be more tolerant of others' faults. Give yourself time to draw from your storehouse and redirect your thoughts to more positive ones. Once you have redirected, enter yourself back into the situation. It is more likely you will make sound decisions based off of reasons and not emotions.

When dealing with triggers there is always a hallucination attached to your trigger. What is the hallucination? It is whatever you imagine will happen as a result of your preference not being met. Your mind gives you the worst case scenarios. For example, you come home from work; you see the dishes are not done. You immediately think that your house is going to be infested with insects and rodents because it is dirty. Speak the hallucination out loud. Often it will bring to your mind how ridiculous your hallucination is. Most of the time the reality will be nothing like that. Maybe your wife had to deal with an issue at your son's school that caused her to arrive back home late. She rushed to put dinner in the oven and tidy the house but didn't have time to wash the dishes before you walked in.

Once we have realized our triggers and the stories that come along with them we can work on self-regulation from a point of knowledge instead of settling for frustration with no change. With your new found knowledge of your triggers, you can choose to deal with the trigger and grow or avoid it all together. Either way, you want to be able to respond and not react to the negative triggers in your life.

Another very powerful strategy for increasing your level of self-regulation is to always look at the consequences of the actions you are about to take. How will this affect others in your life on a personal level; family, friends and neighbors? How will this affect your colleagues? How will this affect your employers? Thinking along these lines will allow you to refocus and see the bigger picture. You will have the ability to see pass the moment and look into the long-term. How many situations have you seen, when a decision was made at the spur of the moment or in the heat of anger and it changed the lives of the people involved forever? Don't let this be you.

Starting very young, as early as infancy, we are taught the external reward system. If you do something good then you will receive a good reward. And this system does work externally but only for a moment. This approach will not work in the long term. You must have an internal motivation. You must know your 'why?' What makes you do the things you do? What motivates you to keep going when things get hard? External motivations will not kick you out of your bed in the wee hours of the morning when everyone else is still sleeping. After some time you will begin to make excuses for not accomplishing your goals if all you have is an external reward system in place.

Guess what? If you don't know your why, you will eventually hit a break wall. Frustration and anger can creep in and negative results occur because you have no internal goal set for yourself. In order to increase your level of emotional intelligence you have to know what drives you to succeed.

Now, as we took a look at the first three components of emotional intelligence, we focused on self. But now we will take a look at a component that deals with the other person; empathy. Empathy is the ability to identify the emotions in others, understand how the situation or circumstance affect them and empathize with them. In many relationships, the one thing that destroys them is a lack of empathy on one or both parts.

In your personal life, you have to be concerned with the thoughts and feelings of the other person. Each person's thoughts and feelings must be valued even if they are the opposite of your own. As individuals, you will not always agree, you are not bound to or expected to. So when situations arise, try to understand where the other person is coming from. It is not about always being right. There will be times you have to make decisions based on the other person's point of view. And this is where a lot of trouble comes in for some people. If one person's point of view or feelings are not being validated, then the other person begins to feel ignored and devalued. Once this happens, even if you don't realize it, the relationship is on the decline. The relationship suffers a lot of damage and in some cases becomes the sole reason for a breakdown and breakup in the relationship. Things may not have come to that point had each person considered the other.

In the workplace having empathy is important. You are constantly dealing with a myriad of people, personalities and cultures. This can prove challenging but taking time to listen to your coworkers, teammates, or bosses and taking their points of view into consideration before making any decisions can make your professional environment peaceful and give those around you a feeling of inclusiveness. You never want the people you work with to feel like they are not part of the team or that their contributions to the time don't matter.

John Donne stated in his work *Devotions Upon Emergent Occasions and Seuerall Steps in my Sicknes - Meditation XVII, 1624* "no man is an island."

> **"No man is an island entire of itself; every man is a piece of the continent, a part of the main;"- John Donne**

Stop acting as if you are and island; shying away from others or treating them as if they don't exist. When you treat people in this manner, you will find you are alone most of the time. You will also find that when you need someone to be empathetic and understand with your situation, they won't. Here are some ways to become more empathetic:

- Pay attention to what is going on with the other person, physically and mentally.

- Listen intensively without concerning yourself with what your response is going to be. Strive for understanding first. Use active listening skills, letting the person know that you hear and understand what is being said.

- Always respond in an encouraging manner. Even if the content is not favorable. You never want to discount a person, his situation, or his ideas altogether.

- Be flexible and approachable. Having an open door policy will assist with this. Let people know that they can come to you at any time for assist or to talk things out. And be ready to receive them.

- Be ready to change as you learn others thoughts and feelings. As you begin to learn about the people around you and their ideas; you just may find that you need to change some things and be ready to do so.

The Origins of Emotional Intelligence

Many people think that emotional intelligences is a new concept. But Plato stated connected learning to emotions. He spoke of this connection over 2,000 years ago.

All learning has an emotional base. - Plato

Since that time people have been studying and asking the same questions. Does emotion have a place in the world of intellect? Most psychologists, philosophers, and common folk have considered intelligence alone to be the judge of how well someone can take, store, and use information. The popular thought was that emotions got in the way of the intellect and had no place in the world of academia and the workplace. In fact, displaying emotions was seen as a form of weakness. Intelligence may be the judge of how someone can store information but what about what they choose to do with this information. How do they transfer that knowledge on to others? How do they apply their knowledge to everyday situations? That, my friend, is emotional intelligence.

Each century there has been psychologists and great thinkers to pop up and back the field of emotional intelligence. Although leaders in education and professional arenas held on to the idea that IQ determined success, there were too many examples to show otherwise. Many with high IQ's were not successful as some predicted while others with less education and lower IQ went on to become very successful.

In the 1920's, Edward Thorndike took his research beyond general intelligence. He called it social intelligence, and described it as "the ability to understand and manage men and women, boys and girls and to act wisely in human relations.

P.E. Vernon elaborated on the definition of social intelligence in the 1930's. He said it was "the ability to get along with people in general, social technique or ease in society, knowledge of social matters and susceptibility to stimuli from other members of a group, as well as insights into the temporary moods or underlying personality traits of strangers."

There was not much said about emotional intelligence in the 1940's but in the 1950's Abraham Maslow, famous for his hierarchy of needs brought a concept to the forefront for the first time. He proposed that people, unlike IQ, could build emotional strength and could develop the ability to effectively handle and control emotions. After Maslow brought this concept into the spotlight, great thinkers and psychologists have studied, developed and expounded on emotional intelligence.

Going into the 70's and through the 80's there was a lot of groundbreaking work done in the field of social intelligence, which emotional intelligence is a branch of. Howard Gardner, an American cognitive psychologist, posed that people don't just have a singular intellectual capacity but rather have multiple intelligences. In 1983, Gardner published a book called *Frames of the Mind: The Theory of Multiple Intelligences.* In this great work he stated that people have 8 different intelligences and suggested that there might be a 9th.

Although Gardner's theory received a lot of criticism especially among psychologists, his theory became popular among educators. Before this time the educational system, especially in America, was a 'one-size-fits all' system built of mostly rote memorization. The sum total of a good American education was how much information you could store and regurgitate. There was no room for variation. There was no striving on the part of the teacher to learn the student or consider the child may have a different way of taking in information.

> **"The less a person understands his own feelings, the more he will fall prey to them. The less a person understands the feelings, the responses, and the behavior of others, the more likely he will interact inappropriately with them and therefore fail to secure his proper place in the world."**
> — *Howard Gardner*

Once Gardner introduced his 8 categories of intelligences, educators and school systems began adjusting educational programs toward different learning styles and intelligences. His theory forever changed the way educational pedagogy was played out in the classroom. A student who was once labeled 'learning disabled' was now kept in mainstream classrooms instead of isolated into separate classes with other children who were classified as 'slow learners.' Teachers began providing scaffolds that catered to different intelligences. For once the intellectual quotient was being questioned and other intelligences were being highlighted. The intelligences proposed by Gardner are as follows:

- Visual-spatial intelligence

- Linguistic-Verbal Intelligence

- Logical-Mathematical Intelligence

- Bodily-Kinesthetic Intelligence

- Musical Intelligence

- Interpersonal Intelligence

- Intrapersonal Intelligence

- Naturalistic Intelligence

All of these intelligences have a part to play in the combination of intellect and emotion. Knowing them and being able to identify them in yourself and others can lead to stronger personal and professional relationships.

Visual-Spatial Intelligence

If you are strong in visual-spatial intelligence then you are good at visualizing things. You can interpret pictures, charts, and graphs well. In the workplace you present information well and are usually an essential part of the team, assisting everyone in seeing the pieces of the puzzle.

Linguistic-Verbal Intelligence

If you are this type of intelligence you are good with words both spoken and written. You memorize well and can relay information to others in a clear and understandable manner. One activity that can increase your emotional intelligence is reading. If you read a myriad of topics especially non-fiction material, it expands your thinking pass its expected boundaries.

Logical-Mathematical Intelligence

For centuries people have praised mathematical minds. Most people considered them to be geniuses. Even in movies, the mathematically inclined are viewed as out of touch with reality and devoid of emotion. Yet they are also portrayed as groundbreaking and inventive. Gardner described the logical-mathematical intelligence as having the ability to analyze and solve problems easily. When you think of emotional intelligence and the workplace, someone with strong analytical skills and an understanding of others is an irreplaceable asset.

Bodily-Kinesthetic Intelligence

There are some people who are more physically inclined than others. They love being physically active In fact; kinesthetic intelligence types are good at doing things. A visual intelligence type may be able to interpret what needs to be done, it is the kinesthetic intelligence who will mobilize and get it done. The more you draw on and recognize different intelligences the more you can increase your emotional intelligence in general.

Musical Intelligence

You always sing and dance. You find patterns and rhythm in things around you. Chances are your strength is with the musical intelligence. Those of you, who are musically inclined, function well with music playing in the background. It helps you to stay focused and uncluttered.

Interpersonal Intelligence

Do you understand and relate to others more than most? If so, you may be an interpersonal intelligent type. You can quickly pickup on others emotions, intentions and desires. Because of this strength, you make a good team lead or manager. You are able to work easily with others nationwide and abroad. You don't know any strangers. You are able to relate regardless of the person. Even if this is not your intelligence type, if you can be work on and increase your interpersonal skills, you will see a major difference in all of your relationships.

Intrapersonal Intelligence

People who have a strong intrapersonal intelligence along with those who have interpersonal intelligence are powerhouses in the work place. This type of person knows his emotions and triggers well. He has a high level of self-awareness and he is good at self-reflection. This is a much needed skill and one that can be improved over time when working on your overall emotional intelligence.

Naturalistic Intelligence

The final intelligence proposed by Howard Gardner is the naturalistic intelligence. People who have this strength are interested in nature and can find the natural patterns in nature. It is also said that even the slightest change in environment can be detected by someone naturally inclined.

Howard Gardner did a lot of research on social intelligence and his categories of intelligences have changed the world of education forever. Most school programs today can contribute part or their entire curriculum to his multiple intelligence theory.

Although the concept of emotional intelligence has been around for many years, the actual term was not used until 1990 by two psychologists named Peter Salovey and John Mayer. They published an article titled *Emotional Intelligence* in the journal *Imagination, Cognition, and Personality*.

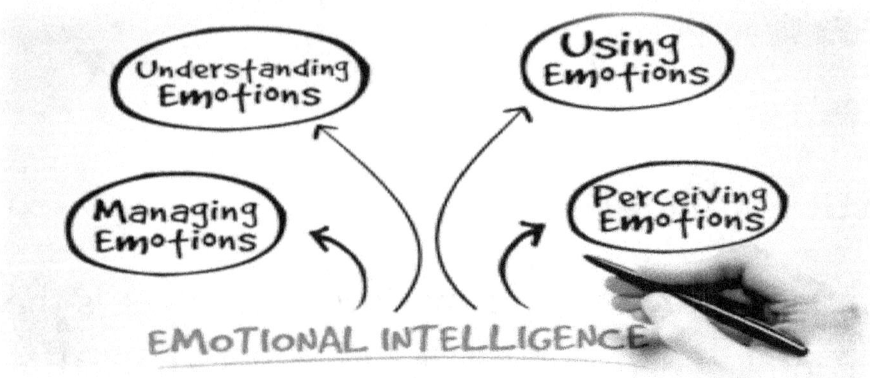

Salovey and Mayer define emotional intelligence as "the ability to engage in sophisticated information processing about one's own and others' emotions and the ability to use this information as a guide to thinking and behavior. That is, individuals high in emotional intelligence pay attention to, use, understand, and manage emotions, and these skills serve adaptive functions that potentially benefit themselves and others". These men went on to divide emotional intelligence into four levels:

- Perceiving emotions
- Reasoning with emotions
- Understanding emotions
- Managing emotions

These four intelligence skills fall under two competencies: personal competence and social competence. Personal competence consists of self-awareness and self-management skills. It's all about you and your ability to stay on top of your emotions and manage your behaviors. Social competence consists of social awareness and relationship management skills. These two intelligences are about how you relate to the people around you. Mayer and Salovey stated that in order for a person to be emotionally intelligent he must possess all of these levels of emotional intelligence.

> ***The emotionally intelligent person is skilled in four areas: identifying emotions, using emotions, understanding emotions, and regulating emotions. – John Mayer***

Being able to perceive your emotions correctly is important. There is no way to understand others if you don't understand yourself. Mayer and Salovey stated that the first stage of perceiving emotions is to actually know what you are feeling in the moment and understand your tendencies across situations. This includes your thoughts and emotions. To obtain a high degree of self-awareness, you must be willing to tolerate the discomfort of focusing on feelings that may be negative. Once you have taken a hold of your own emotions you have the ability to enter into the next stage, which is being able to understand other people's feelings and thoughts. With these skill sets locked in, you will have the ability to express your emotions and differentiate between appropriate and inappropriate emotional expressions.

The second level of emotional intelligence is the reasoning phase.

You must be able to take the emotions you are feeling and reason with them. Take them through a thought process so to speak. In the first phase your emotions guide your thoughts to the most important information. Sometimes you may get bogged down with random thoughts and they need to be weeded out. As you begin to sort through your thoughts and emotions they begin to intensify and at this point you can really identify them. Situations that create strong emotions will require more thought, however, the deep reflection that strong emotions require will keep you from doing something that you regret. Reaching the point of really knowing and sorting through your emotions, you are able to observe and think about others points of view and let that guide you into making good decisions.

Understanding your emotions can be difficult. But when you allow yourself to go through the process it is life changing. In the beginning, you struggle to understand your emotions, where they come from, what triggered them, and how to deal with them. But once you begin to really understand your emotions, you will have the ability to identify and interpret complex emotions as well as transitions between those emotions.

Managing your emotions takes some work. Once you have identified them, know which ones are important and whether they are negative or positive, you can begin to regulate and manage your emotions. The negative ones you keep in check and the positive ones you increase. People high in self-awareness are remarkably clear in their understanding of what they do well, what motivates and satisfies them, and which people and situations push their buttons. This is your goal.

Why Emotional Intelligence can matter more than Intelligence Quotient

In 1990, Daniel Goleman came across an article by Peter Salovey and John Mayer on emotional intelligence. And in 1995, Goleman wrote a book titled *Emotional Intelligence: Why It Can Matter More than IQ*. He believed that emotional intelligence was a better judge of future success than the then popular intelligence quotient testing that was prevalent during that time. His ideas were met with some resistance but his work brought the subject of emotional intelligence to the public eye.

We have done a lot of talking about intelligence and placed a rather large spotlight on emotional intelligence. There are many who question which one matters the most, emotional intelligence or the intelligence quotient, better known as IQ. In order to come up with an answer for this question, let's take a look at them, define them and see exactly what they cover.

Intelligence in its simplest definition is how smart or clever you are. The intelligence quotient or IQ for short is a measurement of intelligence and represented by a number. This number is derived from a battery of standardized tests that also consider age in the grading factor. IQ testing only considers the cognitive ability of an individual as a whole and many believe it is too narrow a determiner to judge actual intellectual ability because it does not take into consideration any emotional or social aspects. IQ testing determines quantitative reasoning, working memory and short-term memory, fluid reasoning, and visual and spatial processing.

As previously mentioned, emotional intelligence is a person's ability to recognize his emotions and the impact they have on others and being able to regulate those emotions in your daily relationships. Also emotional intelligence is the ability to read the emotions of the people around you, understand how they affect them, empathize with them and be able to handle the relationship appropriately. Emotional quotient is the measurement of a person's level of emotional intelligence.

Intelligence quotient used to be the sole determinant of a person's success. But, how many people do you know who are superior intellectually but they are always in some kind of social or emotional dilemma? We see it all too often. Colleagues who have no friends, eat alone on lunch breaks, and are never invited to the company events because they have little or no social skills and make every situation seem odd. This is because his emotional quotient is low. He doesn't have the social skills to be able to blend with his peers. His personal relationships suffer for the same reason.

If your emotional abilities aren't in hand, if you don't have self-awareness, if you are not able to manage your distressing emotions, if you can't have empathy and have effective relationships, then no matter how smart you are, you are not going to get very far.- Daniel Goleman

In order to have beneficial and productive relationships personally and professionally, you must be able to relate to others. In this aspect, emotional intelligence matters more than intelligence quotient. Many times a person with an average IQ becomes insanely successful. It seems that everyone loves him and he climbs the ladder of success quickly in the workplace. This is because although he may have an average IQ, he has an above average EQ. He is able to relate to others, make decisions based on knowledge of the people around him on a deeper level than others.

Many times a person with a high IQ lands a magnificent job, but he doesn't stay in his position long because he is not emotionally intelligent. Having a high IQ lets us know that you have a good grasp on concepts and abstract ideas. But this is not what makes you successful in the workplace. You work with people, not abstract ideas. The success of your company rests on the combination of the efforts of everyone in your organization. If there a lot of misunderstandings, communication errors, and various emotional tensions, the quality of work will be reduced and projects will begin to fail. It takes members of the team having an understanding of themselves and the people who that work with for things to run smoothly. That is why many corporations today include emotional and social intelligence for their employees

Chapter 2: Emotional Intelligence and Cognitive Behavioral Therapy

In today's world there are so many different situations that pull at the emotions of an individual. It is important that we learn to respond to our emotions in a positive way. In this book we have taken a look at emotional intelligence; being able to identify your emotions, the emotions in others and respond to them appropriately. We have explored the levels of emotional intelligence, the need to have emotional intelligence and how a person can increase his emotional intelligence. Because we live in a world full of social ills, there are many who have emotional breaks and dysfunctions that disturb the quality of their daily lives. In the rise of these emotional dysfunctions, various psychologists have created therapies to identify problems and techniques to bring about a solution to these issues. This is where cognitive behavioral therapy comes in.

It's all in your head?

Cognitive behavioral therapy is a form of psychotherapy. It was invented by a psychiatrist named Aaron Beck. He found that the link between feelings and thoughts was important and came up with the term automatic thoughts. Automatic thoughts are usually associated with intense emotional states like depression, anxiety, anger, and euphoria. There are several characteristics of automatic thoughts:

- They are internal dialogues that carry specific messages.

- They appear as short messages by way of keywords.

- They are involuntary thoughts. They are hard to control and hard to avoid.

The therapy Beck invented helps patients to understand the thoughts and feelings that may be influencing their behaviors. It treats problems by modifying dysfunctional feelings, thought patterns and behaviors. The concept of cognitive behavioral therapy is based on the fact that thoughts, feelings, and actions are interconnected and that negative thoughts can trap you into a cycle of non-productive and sometimes destructive behaviors.

"Cognitive therapy seeks to alleviate psychological tensions by correcting misconceptions. By correcting erroneous

beliefs, we can end the overreactions."- Aaron Beck

Cognitive behavioral therapy is popular for a couple of reasons. Many therapy programs last for quite some time. Some programs last for years. But cognitive behavioral therapy is short-term. It works on a specific emotional dysfunction; identifying it, understanding its source, and working on solutions to deal with that particular emotion and the behaviors that come along with it. Another reason cognitive behavioral therapy is popular is because the therapist is very active in the treatment of the patient. It is a one-on-one sort of treatment where the treatment plan is discussed and planned directly with the patient. There are no other therapists or co-patients involved. There are many people who do not want others involved in what they see as their personal lives. So working directly with a therapist is appealing.

What is the goal of cognitive behavioral therapy?

The goal of cognitive behavioral therapy is to assist the client in identifying distorted or irrational thinking patterns. Once the client has identified these patterns, it helps them to control the emotions and behaviors that stem from these thoughts. Often a client has dealt with dysfunctional thoughts and assumptions for so long that they actually don't know where they come from. Many negative thoughts are deep rooted in childhood and have become a part of a person's automatic thoughts. For example, a small girl is told not to overeat because she is becoming fat and when she gets older people will not like her if she's fat. This girl grows up with anxiety every single time she begins to eat. She loves the way the food tastes but wants people to love her. So she begins a dangerous pattern of overeating and throwing up. She becomes unhealthy simply because she believes no one will love her if she carries extra pounds. The goals in her sessions would be to change her thought pattern with food, change her thoughts about her self-image, promoting self-love and self-care. Overall the goal of therapy is to change patterns of thinking or behavior that are behind people's difficulties, and so change the way they feel.

What happens in a therapy session?

A therapy session is usually scheduled once per week or every two weeks. These sessions last between 30-60 minutes and are very specific in nature. Cognitive behavioral therapy sessions are different than other more traditional therapy session. Remember cognitive behavioral therapy is very specific and goal-oriented. So there is no sitting in front of the therapist; rambling on and on about things that come to your mind. During the first sessions you and the therapist will separate your problems into different categories; thoughts, physical feelings and actions. The next stage would be to work out whether these areas are unrealistic or unhelpful. From there you will determine how these areas affect you.

After that, the therapist will be better able to create a treatment plan that is doable for you. The first thing that your provider would want to change is harmful and unhelpful behaviors and thoughts. Once you have worked out these kinks, your therapist will ask you to practice different scenarios at home and eventually graduating to applying the newly learned techniques to your real life.

Types of Cognitive Behavioral Therapy

The field of cognitive behavioral therapy is not a one size fits all kind of therapy. There are different types of therapies for different situations. We will list some of the most popular ones:

- Rational Emotive Behavior Therapy

- Cognitive Therapy

- Multimodal Therapy

- Dialectical Behavior Therapy

Rational emotive behavior therapy, also known as REBT was developed by a psychologist by the name of Albert Ellis.

"People are not disturbed by things but rather by their view of things."- Albert Ellis

This therapy focuses on self-defeating thoughts in the present. For most part, the way people feel is largely influenced by how they think. When people hold irrational beliefs about themselves or the world, problems can result. The goal of REBT is to help people alter illogical beliefs and negative thinking patterns in order to overcome psychological problems and mental distress. Once these thoughts are identified, the therapist can assist you with evaluating these irrational thoughts and show you how to overcome them. Ellis suggested that people erroneously blame external events for their unhappiness. He stated that it is not the events themselves that cause problems it is out interpretation of those events that cause issues. To explain how this process works, Ellis developed what is called the ABC Model:

- A-Activaing Event: Something happens in the environment around you.

- B-Belief: You hold a certain belief about the event.

- C-Consequence: You have an emotional response to your belief.

REBT uses a variety of tools in treatments such as, self-help books, audio-visual guides, positive visualization and reframing of the mind.

Cognitive therapy focuses on what is in the mind and not so much as the behavior that stems from it. This therapy divides thoughts into three categories: automatic thought, immediate belief, and core belief.

Multimodal therapy was devised my psychologist Arnold Lazarus. The idea behind this therapy is that an individual had different modalities and the therapist must treat the client based on them. Treatment follows seven dimensions of modalities. It is known by its acronym BASIC ID:

- Behavior

- Affect

- Sensation

- Imagery

- Cognition

- Interpersonal relationships

- Drugs/biology

Dialectical behavioral therapy is a type of treatment which teaches clients how to live in the moment. It was originally for clients with borderline personality disorders. Dialectics function based on three main assumptions; all things are interconnect, change is constant and inevitable and opposites can be integrated to form a closer approximation of the truth. So with this therapy the patients and therapist work to resolve the contradiction between self-acceptance and change.

Proven Cognitive Behavioral Therapy Techniques

We now know Cognitive behavioral therapy as a theory. We know in general what happens in session between a therapist and client. But, what are some of the proven techniques clients can take home and use in real world situations? We will discuss 6 major techniques:

- Cognitive Restructuring Technique

- Graded Exposure Assignments

- Activity Scheduling

- Successive Approximation

- Mindfulness Practice

- Skills Training

The cognitive restructuring technique can be employed to understand negative feelings and moods. It allows you to challenge the automatic thoughts in your mind. This technique works well with disorders such as depression, social phobias and relationship issues. Cognitive restructuring is based on 7 concepts originally brought forth in a book entitled *Mind over Mood* by Christine Padesky and Dennis Greenberger. These concepts are as follows:

- Calm Yourself: Use some form of relaxation technique to calm you down from the initial emotion that is upsetting you. (ex. Meditation, deep breathing)

- Identify the Situation: Define the situation that triggered the negative mood or emotion.

- Analyze your Mood: Write down the mood you felt in the middle of that situation. (The mood itself not the thoughts that came along with it.)

- Identify Automatic Thoughts: Write down the automatic thoughts that appeared when you experienced the mood.

- Find Objective Supportive Evidence: Identify any evidence to support these automatic thoughts.

- Find Objective Contradictory Evidence: Identify and write down any evidence that contradicts your automatic thoughts in the situation.

- Identify Fair and Balanced Thoughts: Look at both sides of the situation. Look at your supportive evidence vs. your contradictory evidence. Find the balanced view and write these thoughts down.

- Monitor your Present Mood: Having a clearer view, think and reflect on what you can actually do about the situation.

Graded exposure assignments are one of the most effective techniques in cognitive behavioral therapy; donning a 90% success rate. Many people avoid fearful situations that trigger negative emotions; yet, gradual assigned exposure to these very situations allows a person to overcome their anxiety and fears. As the client masters these emotions, the therapist exposes the client to more difficult situations.

Activity scheduling is a simple technique that works well with patients suffering from depression. In general those who suffer from depression withdraw from others and everyday activities. With activity scheduling, the client uses a chart to record an activity, listing what they did and the intensity of the emotions they felt when doing the activity, their sense of achievement on a scale of 0-10, sense of closeness to others, and the sense of enjoyment the activity brought them. Through this careful evaluation of activities, clients can slowly be re-introduced into daily activities and learn to cope and manage thoughts, moods, and feelings that bring about depression.

Successive Approximation is a technique used to assist people in accomplishing tasks they are overwhelmed by. With this technique you systematically take a large task and break it down into smaller chunks to make the task easier. You can also undertake a similar task with a lower difficulty level. This enables the patient to gradual tackle more complicated or complex tasks without feeling overwhelmed.

Mindfulness is a concept that originated with Buddhism. In its simplest form it means to be in the present moment. When a person is in the present moment, they have no focus on the past or thoughts about the future. When you master mindfulness you don't have an aversion to negative situations or a desire for favorable ones. Mindfulness allows you to focus on the ever-changing nature of life. Nothing stays the same, including ourselves. When you realize on an internal level that you are a being that is ever-changing and evolving, you can release yourself from some of the rigidity and routine you have bound yourself with. You can accept flexibility into your life. The result is less stress and negative emotions.

Skills Training is very important in cognitive behavioral therapy. Many of the problems that arise in relationships personally and in the workplace are because one or both parties have a deficiency when it comes to their social skills. The most common trainings focused on in CBT are assertiveness training, communication training, and social skills training.

Deficits in social skills can be in a variety of areas. The patient may have issues with eye contact, initiating conversation, not knowing appropriate social behavior or knowing the correct social protocols but experiencing anxiety when it comes to their application. Social skills training begins with an in depth evaluation of the client's interpersonal skills deficits. Once the deficits have been identified, the therapist can begin a treatment plan to increase skill use. Usually the therapist likes to use role-play with the client. It gives him an opportunity to practice the skills needed in a safe environment and receive immediate feedback.

Assertiveness training is designed to assist people with standing up for their rights and getting what they deserve from others. People who have problems in with assertiveness fall into two categories:

- Being overly passive and never being able to get what you want and deserve

- Being overly aggressive, getting exactly what you want, but destroying relationships in the process

This therapy is one-on-one with the therapist and highly specific. First the client makes a list of situations where assertiveness was lacking. From this list a hierarchy of assertiveness is created. Together with the therapist, the client begins to work on each situation starting with the least difficult, identifying obstacles for success. The therapist assists the client with the emotional discomfort that comes up when facing these various situations.

Communications skills training once mastered can solve many relationship issues, especially on the job. Communication problems usually involve an issue in listening, speaking, or both. This training can assist the speaker with making himself welcomed and understood to others. One of the ways of doing this is by the speaker using positive statements instead of negative ones. Learning effective listening skills is also paramount. Proper listening skills can help others truly understand the speaker and the speaker feel understood. Some of the listening skills a therapist focuses on are:

- Active Listening

- Rephrasing

- Empathizing

- Validating

- Inquiring

Chapter 3: Self-Confidence

Anytime a person has issues on an emotional level, whether it is depression, social hang-ups, or anxieties; the first advice given is, 'You have to have more confidence.' This is good advice. However, you rarely hear a person go pass that statement. No one tells you how to become more self-confident or how to increase the positive thoughts about your image. In all fairness, most people probably don't know. The majority of people who are self-confident just are. We are a sum total of our experiences and those that we have in our formative years play a large role in how we feel about ourselves. But for someone who is suffering from a lack of confidence, how do they get on the road to self-confidence? What does it mean to be self-confident? What does self-confidence look like? Is self-confidence the same as self-esteem? What about self-efficacy?

What is self-confidence?

A short definition of self-confidence is feeling good about yourself and the world around you. Nice, right? Well, this statement is true. But self-confidence goes deeper than this paper-cut definition you may find in some dictionaries. Self-confidence is actually not a single idea but rather it is a process. This process includes how someone feels about himself and others and how he handles situations even when they are difficult and challenging. Anneli Rufus really hits the nail on the head when she stated self-confidence involves self-respect and having the courage to tell the truth about who you are, what you like, and what you believe. Here are a few examples of what self-confidence looks like:

- Being courageous and standing up for yourself assertively.

- Feeling worthy despite imperfections

- Knowing you are worthy of others' friendship and respect

There are times people have a lack of self-confidence because of their erroneous beliefs concerning what self-confidence is. The set the bar too high when they think that self-confidence is being perfect or having a life free from problems, tests and pains. Being self-confident has absolutely nothing to do with perfectionism and striving for perfection is a sure fire way to set yourself up for a letdown. Self-confidence can be exemplified even when mistakes and failures take place.

Some may confuse self-confidence with self-esteem and self-efficacy. Although these terms are closely related, they are different. Self-confidence is related to how a person feels about himself and others. But self-esteem is internal and it is the degree to which a person values himself. It is not in comparison to anything but how that individual sees himself. And then there is self-efficacy which is someone's belief in his ability to accomplish something. Self-confidence would be a merging of self-esteem and self-efficacy.

A lack of self-confidence can lead to negative emotions that impact a person's quality of life. Some of these feelings are:

- Anxiety

- Depression

- Self-doubt

- Apathy

- Unworthiness

These types of feelings can get a person caught in a vicious cycle of negative emotions and reactive behaviors.

Popular Theories of Self-Confidence

There are many theories of self-confidence in the world of psychology today. One of the oldest among them is Abraham

Maslow's Hierarchy of Fundamental Needs. His theory put forth in 1943 is somewhat outdated but still remains a reference point for the relevance of self-confidence as a fundamental need of every person. Maslow noted that basic needs had to be met before more complex ones could. On his famous pyramid, demonstrating the hierarchy of needs, self-confidence or self-esteem was listed as the second highest level of need. So the essential needs of nutrition, shelter, safety and clothing, etc. must be met before a person can work on his self-confidence level. In later years Maslow modified his hierarchy to include those who had dangerous living situations but still had a high level of self-confidence. His theory is no longer used today as a strict theory but rather a guideline showing how the fulfillment of basic needs can foster in the fulfillment of more complex ones.

Another theory on self-confidence is the Terror Management Theory, also known as TMT. This theory states that self-esteem forms as a way to protect and buffer against anxiety, and people strive for self-confidence and react negatively to anyone or anything that could undermine their worldview beliefs. Those who support this view say that the humans respond with terror to the awareness of their own mortality. The building of self-confidence is the way people inwardly protect themselves from this reality.

A social psychologist by the name of Mark Leary introduced another theory called the Sociometer Theory. This theory suggests that self-esteem is an internal measure of the degree to which one is included or excluded by others. This means that a person's self-confidence or self-esteem level is based on the internal individual perception of social acceptance and rejection. There has been evidence in this field that this may be the case. Social inclusion increases self-esteem while social exclusion decreases it.

The Importance of a Positive Mindset for being Self-Confident

Self-confidence and negativity do not reside in the same zone. These two cannot co-exist. In order to have a nice level of self-confidence, you must have a positive mindset. Part of the Optimist Creed states, 'Promise yourself to talk health, happiness and prosperity to every person you meet.' This statement includes you. You must talk positivity to yourself if you want to be self-confident.

Internal Negativity

All negativity must be cast away. Identify any negative self-talk and replace it with positive affirmations. Here are some examples of negative self-talk that you should never say to yourself:

- I'm not good enough.

- I'm a failure

- I'm too old.

- I'm not smart enough.

- I need to wait until I get everything together.

Never accept the negative connotation that you are not good enough. Don't allow past situations and circumstances keep you stuck in a non-productive place in your life. You can always change the narrative. Know that you are great and you are more than good enough.

You can't hit the mark 100% of the time. But that doesn't mean you are a failure or that you have to accept failure. Always acknowledge what went wrong, reflect, and decide what you could do better the next time around. All people make mistakes along the way. It takes mistakes to know the rights and failures to know success.

Too old! What? There is no such thing? It is never too late to live the life you want to live. There is nothing to stop you from living your purpose, except you. Stop telling yourself this lie. Don't dwell on what you have not accomplished yet. Remember, 'It's your thang, do what you want to do." Do it with love and do it with passion. Author Harry Bernstein wrote 20 books that were never published. His first published novel was in 2007 when he was at the age of 97. He went on to publish another book when he was 98 and yet another when he was 99 years old. Had he accepted defeat or the attitude that he was too old to fulfill his dreams, the world would have never been able to benefit from his works.

Why are you telling yourself that you are not good enough? There is so much information at your fingertips. This cannot be the negative conversation you are having with yourself. Anything you want to know; Google it. You don't know how to do something, search it; I bet there is a YouTube video to show you how it's done. Do you read? If not, try it. Read. Learn something new every day. There are a lot of sites dedicated to knowledge in a myriad of subjects. Educate yourself.

Maybe you are telling yourself that you have to have everything together before you accomplish certain things. Newsflash: You will never find the time when everything is perfect. This is self-talk that keeps you trapped in procrastination and prevents you from accomplishing what you want. Take progressive steps every day and soon you will find that you have met your goals.

External Negativity

The people in your atmosphere must be positive as well. Don't allow negative people and situations to enter your life. They will cause you to doubt everything that is around you and your ability to accomplish anything. If you stay clear of negativity, you will notice that your mindset is more positive. The Optimist Creed also states, 'To be too large for worry, too noble for anger, too strong for fear, and too happy to permit the presence of trouble.' Never let someone else's opinion of you become your reality. Clear your environment of those who don't bring you any benefit.

A positive mindset is the key to building self-confidence.

9 Ways to Increase Self-Confidence

Do you lack self-confidence? Well, the good thing about self-confidence is that it can be increased. It will take some work on your part. Because the way you feel about yourself is deeply rooted and many of those feelings may have developed early in your childhood. So be prepared for the work, know that it can be done and watch your self-confidence grow.

- Sit or stand in a position of confidence. Power poses change the way that you feel about yourself. Amy Cuddy, a Harvard psychologist, stated that studies show that confident body postures hormonally change the way we feel about ourselves. An example of this would be the 'Wonder Woman' pose. With this pose, your body is open; legs spread apart, hands on hips and chin stuck out.

- Build your capacity for energy. A small amount of stress can give you the energy push you need to get the job done. Don't look this small amount of pressure make you nervous.

Reframe this energy as excitement. Learn to engage with your feelings and expand your presence.

- Practice Mindfulness. Mindfulness is something you can practice at any time and in any place. Become aware of the presence. Begin by observing your body beginning with your feet and work your way up to your head. Breathe carefully, slowly and intently. Allow your eyes to become aware of the things in your visual field. Allow your ears to hear the things in your immediate environment. Once you are aware and in the present, go beyond your simple environment to feel quiet, energy or noises around you.
- Use Visualization. Close your eyes and imagine you are confidently standing in whatever situation you want to be more confident in. Allow yourself to experience feelings of comfort and ease.

- Exercise regularly. Exercising releases endorphins which interact with opiate receptors in your brain which produces a pleasurable state of mind. You will view yourself in a more positive light. Not only will you feel better mentally but your physical health will also improve.

- Give yourself permission to take risks and make mistakes. No one has knowledge of every single area. And even when you have knowledge in a particular field, there is always something you can expand on. Allow yourself to be a novice. Soak up information and your confidence level will increase.

- Speak well to Yourself. Having feedback from others has its place. But what about the conversation you are having with self? Always looking to others for feedback and validation is not good. Speak words of encouragement to yourself. The most important relationship you will ever have is the one that you have with yourself. Make it a good one.

- Clarify your Goals. When creating a list of goals you would like to accomplish, start with the larger goals and then create actionable steps to attain each one.

- Ask for help and offer our help to others. No man can live in this world alone. It takes getting help from others at times to success. There is nothing wrong with reaching out for assistance. Your self-confidence level will also increase dramatically if you reach out to help others. It gives you a sense of accomplishment and being a part of the greater good.

If you really put in the work and practice the techniques listed above. You will find your self-confidence getting stronger. You will gain more resilience and self-reliance to tackle anything that comes your way.

Chapter 4: Self-Discipline

Self-discipline is one of the important ingredients to success. In fact, it is important in every area of your life. Having self-discipline gives you the decision making power and determined longevity to follow your decisions through until the end. It enables you to have resolve.

What is self-discipline?

According to Collins dictionary, self-discipline is the ability to control yourself and to make yourself work hard or behave in a particular way without needing anyone else to tell you what to do. Self-discipline has to be present in order for you to accomplish your goals. It gives you the ability to see your decisions and plans through until you accomplish your goals. It is the foundation for your success because it is the key to you getting up and going forward even when you don't want too. It is continuing when you feel like quitting. Self-discipline has nothing to do with how you feel because many days you may not feel like going through the process that you must go through to accomplish things in your life. But self-discipline pushes you through.

What does self-discipline look like?

Self-discipline can be expressed in many ways. There is no way to list all of the ways in this book. So, I will list some of the most common examples of self-discipline.

- Self-control

- Perseverance

- Trying over and over again until you accomplish your goal

- The ability to resist temptations

- The ability to forego immediate satisfaction for the accomplishment of a goal sometime in the future.

Having these skill sets mean completing projects, accomplishing goals, and persevering through all situations. But why do a lot of people have an issue with self-discipline? He has a lot to do with the erroneous beliefs people hold about what self-discipline is.

What Self-discipline is not

When a lot of people think of self-discipline, what comes to mind is limitations and lifestyle restrictions. TV shows and movies have assisted in this narration. Movies contain characters that live in some remote place, with restrictive self-imposed laws, eating only what he can catch or grow. You watch him live an austere life off the beaten path. Towards the end of the show, you see him fulfilling all the goals he has set for himself, non-supporters of his call become avid supporters, and he completely rocks. This is not self-discipline. This is living a life of rigidity as a lifestyle choice. You may even say it is a lifestyle preference. What happens when people have similar narrations in their minds concerning self-discipline, it seems hard to obtain. It seems out of the ordinary. But self-discipline is very attainable and is something that can be perfected.

Positive Mindset and Self-Discipline

Having and positive mindset and having self-discipline go hand-and-hand. It is impossible to acquire self-discipline if you have negative narrations, thoughts, and strongholds in your mind. You have to tell yourself a different narrative. You must plan your goals knowing that you can accomplish them.

Many times we set goals for ourselves and they are unrealistic because we have no plan. You have to couple a positive mindset with actionable steps and the application of self-discipline to realize our goals.

The Power of Habits

In its simplest definition, a habit is a routine behavior. Our routine behaviors can be positive or negative. Habits are recurrent and often unconscious and they are established by repetition. Habits define our character, our thoughts and feelings.

When these habits are negative, they sabotage our progress and growth. And can ultimately prevent us from accomplishing our goals. When habits are positive they can be instrumental in solidifying our self-determination to accomplish the things we want to do.

We have already stated that in goal setting, self-determination is paramount to accomplishing your goals. In order to obtain the type of self-determination you need to realize your goals, good habits aimed at these goals must be formed.

But how do habits work? In the book *The Power of Habits,* Charles Duhigg explains this. He stated that every habit had a three step loop:

- The Cue

- The Routine

- The Reward

So first there is a cue or a trigger that tells your brain to go into automatic mode and also tells you what habit to use. After that initial step, then there is the routine. This routine can be physical, emotional, or mental. The final step is the reward. This helps your brain sort out whether this loop is worth remembering for the future. The more the habit is repeated the more automatic it becomes.

Now when establishing new goals, there are two things you need to do. You need to establish new habits that will support your efforts and get rid of bad habits that will sabotage them. There are some things you can do to establish new habits:

- Start with small steps

- Make the habit daily with no exceptions, no excuses

- Be motivated about the reward

- Set targets and timeframes; reward yourself if you have met your target.

- Be accountable for any fails

- Visualize your rewards

Getting rid of bad habits would be nice. But it's not that easy. You can't just get rid of your bad habits. In order to do away with bad habits you have to change them by changing the routine. Keep the cue and the reward in place but establish a new routine.

Successful People vs. Unsuccessful People

If you observe the lives of successful people as well as unsuccessful people, you will notice some big differences. What do successful people have that is not present in the lives of unsuccessful people? Good Habits and Self-Discipline. We will take a closer look at these differences:

- Giving others vs. Getting for yourself: Successful people consistently give to others. They give of their time, knowledge, and experience. You will find them to be kind in general. Unsuccessful people are always have the 'me' factor before their eyes.

- Positive Mindset vs. Negative Mindset: Successful people have positive attitudes. They spread this positivity wherever they go and with whomever they speak with. It's like their positivity is contagious. Those who are not successful concentrate on what they don't have, what went wrong, who is at fault, what belongs to them, etc.

- Listening vs. Talking: Successful people are always listening. They allow others to talk and consider their ideas. Unsuccessful people usually talk all of the time. They don't listen to others because they are striving to be heard.

- Self-Awareness vs. Self-centeredness: A trait that you will find in all successful people is that they have a high level of self-awareness. They know exactly who they are, what they want, and why they do the things that they do. Most unsuccessful people are unsure of who they are. They are constantly drawing people to themselves.

- Taking chances vs. Being afraid of failure: You will find those who are successful don't mind taking risks in order to accomplish what they want. Unsuccessful people are afraid of taking chances because they are afraid to fail. Successful people realize that through mistakes they learn and grow.

- Always Learning vs. Flying by the Seat of Their Pants: Successful people are constantly learning and at the top of their fields. They grow professionally and personally by obtaining knowledge. They read, attend conferences and take courses. While unsuccessful people put so much time into working that they don't make time to add new skills sets or learn new information.

- Accepting responsibility vs. Blaming others: Successful people accept responsibility for their actions, even when they make mistakes. They take the lesson from the experience and continue building on their self-confidence and management skills. Unsuccessful people always have a sob story to tell. They always have someone to blame for their lack of success.

- Ideas vs. People: Those who are enjoying the fruits of their labor are constantly talking about their ideas and the ideas of others. But unsuccessful people like to carry tales and gossip about the affairs of others.

10 Proven Methods to Master Self-Discipline

If you lack the self-discipline to see things through or to persevere until you accomplish your goals, things can change. The good news is that a skill such as self-discipline can be taught. Through several actionable steps you can increase your level of self-discipline and accomplish the things that you desire. Let's take a look at some of the proven methods of mastering self-discipline:

- Know your weaknesses: Acknowledge your shortcomings. You cannot overcome them until you do. Don't pretend that the shortcomings don't exist and don't try to cover them up either.

- Set Clear Goals and Create and Execution Plan: If you want to achieve self-discipline you have to have a clear picture of what you want to accomplish. Create a mantra to keep yourself focused.

- Remove Temptations: Remove the biggest temptations from your environment; you will increase your self-discipline. Set yourself up for success.

- Create New Habits; Keep it Simple: Break your goals into doable steps. Don't try to change everything at one time, focus on establishing a new habit consistently and master self-discipline.

- Remove subconscious obstacles: Sometimes our resolve and willpower is effective by our own viewpoint. If you believe that there is a limit to your willpower, then there surely is. Don't limit yourself. No that your willpower and self-discipline has no limits and walk in that truth every day.

- Keep a backup plan: Give yourself a plan just in case difficult situations arise. If you have a backup plan you are not forced to make sudden decisions in an emotional state. It is all about self-control.

- Reward yourself: Anticipation is powerful. Build a reward system into your goal planning. It gives you something to look forward to when you accomplish certain tasks.

- No Guilt; No Shame; Forgive yourself and Move On: There will be mistakes on the path to accomplishing your goals. Do not allow yourself to get stuck in the guiling or shaming game. Evaluate the situation, see what caused the mistake, take ownership of it and move on. Do not dwell on it. Guilt is the enemy of progress. This is where your self-discipline kicks in and pushes you to continue on.

If you are serious about mastering self-discipline, work on the methods listed above. You will find through strengthening your self-discipline that in no time you will accomplish your goals.

Chapter 5: Emotional Quotient

Throughout this book we have been exploring emotional intelligence. We have taken a look at what it is and what it is not. We have also taken a look at skill sets that you must have to have a high level of emotional intelligence. We have learned many new terms along the way and there may have been some confusion over the terms emotional intelligence and emotional quotient. There may be some who have wondered what exactly what is EQ and IQ. So we will delve further into these areas.

Emotional quotient is a measure of the emotional intelligence level of an individual, which demarcates between different feelings and use this intelligence to guide thinking and behavior. This term was first used in 1995 by Daniel Goleman. He used it in his book entitled *Emotional Intelligence.* He described emotional quotient as the ability of a person to identify, express and control his/her thoughts and actions, understand other people and rightly interpret their situations, make right and quick decisions and cope with pressures and crisis.

There term intelligence quotient has been around for a long time. It is better known for its acronym, IQ. IQ is an intelligence test score. It is a measure of an individual's intelligence level. IQ is obtained through a standardized intelligence test. The score is derived from an individual's mental age being divided by his chronological age and then multiplied by 100.

Differences between Emotional Quotient and Intelligence Quotient

There are some key points of difference between EQ and IQ that are worthy to note here:

- EQ is the measure of a person's emotional intelligence and IQ is a measure of an individual's logical reasoning ability.

- A person's IQ level determines his success in the world of academia but EQ determines his success in real life.

- Emotional Quotient is acquired and improved. It can increase with training. As opposed to intelligence quotient is an ability you are born with.

- EQ is a person's social and emotional competency. While IQ is a person's academic competency and reasoning ability.

- A person with good EQ can recognize, control and express his own emotions, perceive and assess other's emotions. A person with a high IQ can learn, understand and implement knowledge, and possesses logical reasoning and abstract thinking.

Both EQ and IQ are important. But for overall success in relationships whether they are personal or work-based, EQ is the most important. Your IQ may land you the job. But your EQ will be the factor that allows you to remain on the job successfully. One of the forerunners in this field, Daniel Goleman also spoke about EQ and its importance in children. He felt that all children should have emotional and social learning. Most of the problems that happen in the school environment are emotional or social in nature. If children have been given training in emotional intelligence, they have the internal tools to deal with bullies, cliques, and exclusive behaviors from others. It also gives them additional learning abilities that they would most likely not have obtained in their formative years.

Because of Goleman's thoughts on children and emotional intelligence, many schools have implemented new curriculum and programs to strengthen student's emotional intelligence.

10 Methods to Improve your Emotional Quotient

As has been stated numerous times, emotional quotient is not static. Through education and training, a person's EQ can be increased. You can check with your human resources department to see if they have any programs available to you at work or you can seek a therapist who specialized in emotional intelligence training. Here are some ways that you can increase your emotional quotient:

- Assertive Communication: Learn to communicate in a direct way, still respecting others. Assertiveness is neither passive nor aggressive. There four assertive communication skills; direct eye contact, body posture, modulated voice level, timing. Also using 'I' statements is powerful. It shows that you take ownership

- Respond to Conflict: No emotional outbursts. It is easy turning times of conflict to react to the emotions. Focus on resolutions.

- Active Listening Skills: Listen for clarity; understand what is being said, and pay attention to non-verbal communication. Once you have done this, then you respond.

- Motivation: Emotionally intelligent people are self-motivated and their attitude motivates others. They set goals and are resilient when faced with challenges.

- Maintain a Positive Attitude: Know the attitudes and personalities of the people around you. When you are able to read them, you understand what you need to say and do to have a positive attitude.

- Practice Self-Awareness: Emotionally intelligent people are aware of their emotions and how they impact others.

- Take critique well: Don't get offended or response defensively. Listen to the critique, understand where the critique is coming from, evaluate the situation and see where you can improve on it, and search for resolutions.

- Empathize: Empathy helps to relate to others on a basic human level. Others gain a mutual respect and understanding even if they have differing opinions and situations.

- Utilize Leadership Skills: Take initiative. Use your decision making and problem-solving skills. Set standards and be the example that others can follow

- Be Approachable and Social: Always smile and give off a positive presence. Don't be the one that others are afraid to walk pass your office. Be social and show that you actually care.

Some of these behaviors may already come natural to you, while others may be a little more difficult. Practice being more self-aware and conscious of your interactions with others around you and you will be on the path to increasing your emotional intelligence.

Chapter 6: General FAQ's

1. What is emotional intelligence?

Emotional intelligence is a form of social intelligence that involves knowing your own emotions and the feelings and emotions of others. This information is then used to guide one's thinking and actions.

2. What does emotional intelligence entail?

Emotional intelligence has four core abilities: zeal and persistence, self-control, self-motivation, and empathy for oneself and others.

3. Who invented the term emotional intelligence?

Peter Salovey and John Mayer coined the phrase emotional intelligence in 1990. The term was made popular by Daniel Goleman in his book titled *Emotional Intelligence.*

4. Can emotional intelligence be developed?

The short answer is, yes. There are many techniques that can be learned to develop the core aspects on emotional intelligence.

5. How is emotional intelligence developed?

Emotional intelligence can be developed through didactic instruction, role modeling, and direct experience.

6. Why is emotional intelligence important?

It is important to for professional and personal relationships to be able to know yourself and the people around you. Many of the problems in today's workforce stem from a breakdown in communication.

75 percent of careers are derailed for reasons

7. Why have we just begun to hear about this term in recent years?

This term has been surfacing in recent years due to the hard work of researchers, psychologists, and trainers. Some of the researchers foremost in this field are Peter Salovey, John Mayer, and Daniel Goleman. Society typically downplays emotions and refers to people who display their emotions as being weak.

8. What role do our emotions play day to day?

Emotions govern our actions. From the time we wake up until the time we go to bed our emotions affect our every action.

9. What mistakes have we been making?

We reject negative emotions because they are painful or uncomfortable. We often do this with children. When a child has a temper tantrum, we say things like, 'be a big girl, grow up.' This invalidates the child's feelings and sends the message that in order to be a strong person you can never cry.

10.   Is sadness and anger healthy?

Yes. All emotions we experience are in our lives for a reason. Every emotion has something to teach us. Emotional intelligence is not about getting rid of negative emotions all together. It is about knowing how to manage them when they occur and know how to regulate them so that they don't impact our relationships in a negative way.

11.   What skills help develop emotional intelligence?

Rapidly reduce stress

Develop emotional awareness

Improve non-verbal communication

Use humor to deal with challenges

Resolve conflict positively

12.   Why are we speaking about emotions in the context of
business?

Emotions drive behavior. If a boss wants an employer to
change his behavior, he has the appeal to that person's
emotions. When employees work as a team, it is their
emotional intelligence that determines the success of that
union and whether projects are completed successfully.

13.   What are the characteristics of someone with high
emotional intelligence?

Emotionally intelligent people are not afraid of change, in
fact, they welcome it.

They are self-aware. They know what they are good at and
they know their weaknesses. Weaknesses do not scare
them.

A person with high emotional intelligence is empathetic. He
knows the feelings of others, can relate to them, empathize
with them, and work through difficult times with ease.

Empathy is one of the main concepts that are focused on in the field of emotional intelligence.

They realize perfectionism is impossible. They take their mistakes, learn from them, and keep it rolling.

Emotionally intelligent people are balanced. They have good work-life balance. They take time to participate in activities outside of the workplace.

They are curious. They look at the world with non-judgmental eyes and are always prepared to learn new things.

14.   How can emotional intelligence assist children?

For so many years IQ has been focused on in the school environment while year after year, the social and emotional conditions of the children progressively worsened. Children who have emotional intelligence education are better equipped to deal with issues like peer pressure, bullying, depression, and adolescent uncertainty.

Conclusion

Thank you for making it through to the end of *Emotional Intelligence: The Ultimate Guide for Cognitive Behavioral Therapy (CBT), How to Analyze People, Success at Work, Better Life & Relationships with Positive Psychology Mindset Coaching 2.0*, let's hope it was informative and able to provide you with all of the tools you need to achieve your goals whatever they may be. In a world of people full of unregulated emotions, a book like this is paramount. There is no area of your life that you don't have to deal with emotions, negative and positive.

In this book we covered emotional intelligence and its importance in society today. We looked at emotional intelligence compared to other intelligences, its history, and how a person can increase his emotional intelligence in order to deal with the many relationships he deals with on a daily basis. Knowing how to identity and control your own emotions as well as know the emotions of others is crucial.

The next step is to try some of the techniques that were mentioned in this book to improve your emotional intelligence. If you don't feel comfortable practicing these methods on your own, begin searching for a therapist who specializes in this field. Set up an appointment and change everything in your life by working on your emotional intelligence level.

Finally, if you found this book useful in any way, a review on Amazon is always appreciated!

THANK YOU